The Fight

of

The Faith

The Fight

of

The Faith

T. Austin-Sparks

LIFE SENTENCE Publishing, LLC

THE FIGHT OF THE FAITH

ISBN 13: 978-0-9832016-1-8

Available from the Publishers at:

LIFE SENTENCE Publishing, LLC
404 N 5th Street
Abbotsford, WI 54405
715-223-3013

www.lifesentencepublishing.com
Please ask questions and discuss this book on our online forum.

Printed in the United States of America

Contents

This series of messages was first published in
"A Witness and A Testimony" magazines, 1942-43

Scripture quotations are from the
American Standard Version of the Bible
(1901), unless otherwise indicated.

Publisher's Note

With the exception of minor corrections, all of this book's content remains unchanged from the original words of T. Austin-Sparks, taken from the website of www.austin-sparks.net.

In keeping with T. Austin-Sparks' wishes, this book is available for free at www.lifesentencepublishing.com. Please continue to respect T. Austin-Sparks' wishes in that what was freely received should be freely given. We ask, as is asked on the website, that if you choose to share this book with others, that you please respect his wishes and offer them freely – free of changes, free of charge, and free of copyright.

It is our pleasure to bring glory to God's Kingdom by making this book available to those who may otherwise not have received some of the wisdom of Christ through the pen of T. Austin-Sparks.

Jeremiah M. Zeiset
LIFE SENTENCE Publishing, LLC
Wisconsin, US, 2011

Chapter 1

THE FAITH

"Fight the good fight of the faith, lay hold on the life eternal, whereunto thou wast called, and didst confess the good confession in the sight of many witnesses" (1 Tim. 6:12).

"I have fought the good fight, I have finished the course, I have kept the faith" (2 Tim. 4:7).

"Beloved, while I was giving all diligence to write unto you of our common salvation, I was constrained to write unto you exhorting you to contend earnestly for the faith which was once for all delivered unto the saints" (Jude 3).

"I know where thou dwellest, even where Satan's throne is; and thou holdest fast my name, and didst not deny my faith, even in the days of Antipas my witness, my faithful one, who was killed among you, where Satan dwelleth" (Rev. 2:13).

These are four passages out of a considerable number in the New Testament which contain the same phrase. I have jotted down some twenty-seven or twenty-eight of such passages, and there are probably more. The phrase that occurs in them all is this phrase - "*the* faith". "Fight the good fight of the faith": "I have kept the faith": "Contend earnestly for the faith."

Now, wherever that phrase occurs, you will not have to look far for the element of conflict. You will find that conflict is almost invariably associated with that phrase - "the faith". That is to say, the two things always go together in the New Testament, and in true spiritual experience - the fight and the faith, or the faith and the fight.

"Fight the good fight of the faith": "Contend earnestly for the faith": "I have fought... I have kept the faith." Thus, although it will not always be as precisely stated as that, I repeat, that you will not have to look far in the context for the element of conflict when "the faith" is in view.

Of course, that may not be very surprising. It is the sort of thing you would naturally expect to find when anything like a new faith which might be a rival faith to other faiths was being introduced.

The Faith — Not a System of Teaching

But if you look carefully at the matter here in the New Testament, you will find that it is something more than that. The conflict is not occasioned just because another faith which is a rival to existing faiths has been introduced. It is rather in the very nature and essence of this thing that is called "the faith" that the element exists which sets up this terrific conflict. It is something more than just a new religion coming in to challenge and attempt to oust other religions. There is something about this faith which is far more than that, and to grasp and understand what that something more is should be of tremendous help to the Lord's people.

The fact is that the very presence in this world of those who do truly, in a real New Testament way, stand in the faith and have the faith in them - apart from all their framework and form of religion - even without their saying anything about it - constitutes a conflicting factor in the world, and they become centres of spiritual warfare. What I mean is, that you need not announce that you are a Christian, and you certainly need not state your Christian beliefs, in order to be the focal point of antagonism. If you are really in the good of what is meant by "the faith", you are a centre of antagonism. You cannot help it. To try to avoid it is to destroy that essential of the faith.

Thus, in the beginning, the faith was not a system of doctrine or teaching. It was not a number of tenets and truths, but it was a single, though all-inclusive, truth which carried with it a spiritual impact, altogether apart from the defining of that truth.

The New Testament has a wonderful way of summing up everything in very short sentences. We have several of these. For instance, everything at the beginning was gathered into two words - "the way". They were said to be people of "the way". It became a name for them. Or again - "the Name"; everything is gathered into that. Again and again it was the Name. They were commanded "not to teach in this name" (Acts 5:28). They went forth "for the sake of the name" (3 John 7). On many occasions we have it all summarised in that way. It is the Name; very terse, but tremendously significant, boundlessly full: but just two words - "the Name". Or again, on many occasions it is called "the testimony". "Even as the testimony of Christ was confirmed in you" (1 Cor. 1:6); or, as we are so familiar with it in the book of the Revelation - "the testimony of Jesus".

Let me repeat. That was not a systematised doctrine in the first place, a form of teaching, an interpretation of truth. It was something very much more than that, gathered all into very simple, very brief phrases - the Way, the Name, the Testimony, or the Faith. You would be interested and helped if you just went and turned up each of these passages in which this phrase "the faith" occurs and looked at the context.

Well, our point for the moment is this, that there at the beginning the faith was not a doctrine, not something which began and ended with an assent to a statement of truth, even about the Lord Jesus. It was not an embracing of Christianity, an embracing of Christian truth, an embracing of the Christian position. Such phrases have come to mean no more than becoming associated with Christianity and Christians, and subscribing to what they believe.

The Faith — a Spiritual Reality in Terms of Experience

Oh no, it was not that, it was something deeper than that. It was a spiritual reality in terms of an experience. The Faith was an experience: the Name was an experience: the Testimony was an experience: the Way was an experience. Beloved, I want to stress that just for a moment, because, while we are not going to make everything of our experience, everything of Christ has to be an experience. Everything that is true of the Lord Jesus as He stands in relation to us has to have its counterpart in us an experience. His birth has to be an experience, not merely an historical fact. His baptism has to be an experience, on the death side, the burial, the resurrection. It is something that has to be done in us. We have to know in our own history; not in the history of the Lord Jesus, not in the book which is the history of Christ, but in our own history. All has to be as something through which we have passed in a living experience. We have to know that He died; that death has to have a registration in our his tory as something through which we have gone with Him. So also His resurrection; it is to be an experience.

Think you that the coming again of the Lord Jesus is going to be just an historic event in an objective form? While all is true of the Lord Jesus in an historical way, that is not enough for the Church, that is not enough for us. No, His coming again, while it will be actually objective, historical, will be an experience, wrought in the very life, heart and nature of those who are joined with Him. He is not only coming to be manifested in glory, but He is coming to be glorified in the saints (2 Thess. 1:10). Not only objective, but subjective, is the coming of the Lord.

And all other things that are true about Him have to take that character. What a vast difference it would have made from the beginning if the truth of the Church, the Body of Christ, had been kept there. If only all the Lord's people had realised from the beginning, and realised today, that the Church is an experience and not a doctrine. The Body of Christ is an experience, something that goes through you and through which you go. I mean this: in the beginning they had no doctrine of the Body of Christ at all, no teaching about the Church but they had the Church. And how did they have it? I sometimes think they had it in a much more living way than it has been had since the doctrine came. They were in this world as a company of those who stood in isolation from the world; they were Christians, and all the rest of the world were not Christians. There were only two kinds of people on the earth, namely, Christians and non-Christians, and because the Christians were in a minority, and were just a people by themselves, they desperately needed one another. It was a matter of life and death to them whether they had fellowship with other Christians. They could not live without one another. That was the Church. It was an experience.

If all Christians today were unable to live without one another, what a different situation there would be! If only all such realised they belong to the Lord and all the others do not, and that this is the one great difference to be taken account of - You are in Christ or you are not in Christ, and, if you are in Christ, you cannot live without your fellow-members in Christ, you must have one another. If that were true, we would have the Church, the Body, in reality. That is what I mean by saying it is an experience; something wrought at the very heart of us that is really the Church. Would to God we could just step right back there where, because we were so necessary to one another, we could never harbour a spirit of criticism toward one another, because we would be doing ourselves as great an injury as we would be doing to the one criticised. That is an experience.

Now, the faith is that: it is a spiritual reality. The testimony is that; not a doctrine, a teaching, in the first place, but a living experience. It is something which carries with it a power, a spiritual power, and that power registers itself against opposing powers, without any terms, without any phraseology.

The Faith — a Spiritual Position

Then it resolves itself into two things. Firstly, it resolves itself into a spiritual position. The faith is more than a doctrine; it is a spiritual position. Those who are in the faith, and of the faith, are a people who occupy a position which is recognised by all the spiritual intelligences which are in another position, and, because they occupy that position, they are marked out, and without inviting it they know what spiritual conflict is. Their very position brings that upon them.

By way of illustration in the type, the antagonism of the nations toward Israel of old was simply because of Israel's spiritual position. They represented a heavenly position as apart from this world, as in union with God and His Christ, and ultimate supremacy was bound up, not with them just in a people, but with them as a people in the spiritual position which they held. When they lost their spiritual position, the destiny was suspended, the realisation of the purpose was made impossible. But, while they preserved the spiritual position, that, in itself, brought everything against them. You might have said, Well, these people, somehow or other, are the most provocative people in the world; somehow or other they stir up trouble wherever they go! That may be said to their disadvantage, to their discredit, but the fact is that they could not help themselves. It was not that they were inviting hostility, but their very position precipitated it, and brought it upon them.

And we must recognise that there is something even more in the antitype than in the type; I mean in the case of the Church. The Church is a far more spiritual thing than was Israel on the earth. The Church is a far more heavenly thing in reality than was that which was only heavenly in type, and we shall be very provocative people if we are in the faith. I mean that we shall be the cause of trouble; there will be spontaneous antagonism. We shall not have to be awkward people who cannot get on with anybody. We shall be here as a challenge, and we shall not be able to avoid or evade spiritual conflict. It becomes spontaneous.

It is like that in the type. You remember the smitten rock, the waters gushing out, and the Psalm "Spring up, O well" (Num. 21:17) - a foreshadowing of the Holy Spirit coming in fulness into the life of the Lord's people. What is the next thing? "Then came Amalek, and fought with Israel" (Ex. 17:8). There is nothing between. "Spring up, O well": that is one phase. The next phase is, "Then came Amalek, and fought..." Pentecost, then persecution! The Spirit, then the wilderness and the Devil! It is always like that. A spiritual position precipitates spiritual conflict, and the faith was always in that very atmosphere and realm. Every time you have the faith, you have the fight. It is a position.

The Faith — a Nature

But of course it is also another thing. It is a nature. A kind of being has come into God's universe which is not welcome, the universe being as it is. To spoil that kind, to change that nature, will be the one object of those antagonistic forces; to bring down from the position by corrupting, polluting, tainting, changing the nature if possible. That was the enemy's objective in and with the very Son of God Himself in the wilderness; to get Him to forsake His exalted position by coming down on to another level of life and nature.

The faith, then, represents a kind of people who must be got rid of, if possible, anyhow: and therein lies the conflict. So the faith is not just a subject preached or taught; it is a power let loose. That is the faith - a power let loose. Paul says, "I have fought the good fight... I have kept the faith"; and he exhorts Timothy to "fight the good fight of the faith". The article occurring three times in that statement is impressive - "Fight *the* good fight of *the* faith, lay hold on *the* eternal life".

The Principle of Sonship — the Heart of the Faith

This is something specific, unique, peculiar in God's universe, which marks out those associated with it as being different in position and nature, and we must get closer to this, with regard to what the faith was and is. I think the best point at which we can approach it and get help is to note just where the fight came to light. I do not mean where the fight began; it began long, long centuries before this. It began in the Garden; it began perhaps even before the Garden. But, while it was there all the time right through the ages, it came to light in its nature and meaning at a certain point. The Lord Jesus dragged it out into the light by coming Himself, by Himself being present.

In Luke 4 we have the point at which the fight came most clearly to light, and it is couched in this interrogation repeated by the enemy - "If thou be the Son of God..." The occasion was a battle in the wilderness between Christ and Satan, the battle of all the ages now joined in its fullest and deepest and most malignant sense, and that battle is concentrated in this word - "If thou be the Son of God..."

What then, is "the faith"? It is gathered into that phrase "the Son of God". Now, Jesus Christ as the Son of God - that is, the deity of Christ - may be a tenet of the Christian faith, a part of Christian doctrine; but oh, it is something more than that! It is something around which this battle has raged in unabated fury. It is the occasion of all the conflict. Jesus, the Son of God: that is "the faith".

That is something far more than a statement. I have said it is an experience. Sonship is something immense in God's thought, and it is upon this whole question of sonship that the battle rages, both in His case and in ours. If you want to know what the occasion of all the trouble is, it is gathered into one word - sonship; all that that means with God, both for the Lord Jesus and for the many sons whom He is bringing to glory. That word "sonship" carries with it everything that stirs and rouses hell to its depths, and explains all the trouble, all the suffering, all the conflict. It came to light on that point. There had been an announcement made from heaven - "This is my beloved Son" (Luke 3:22). Then, into the wilderness, and to the challenge - "If thou be the Son..." And so intense was the spiritual conflict in the wilderness that angels had to be sent from heaven to minister unto Him.

Well, we may know just a little bit about that. Have you never known spiritual conflict which has made it necessary for the Lord to minister life to you in such a way that, but for it, you could not go on. That ofttimes is the effect of spiritual conflict. His, of course, was an experience far beyond ours, but we share that, and the focal point of it all is just the same in our case as in His - although He was the consummate centre of it all - sonship. "If thou be the Son..."

In that challenge and that language, there is a recognition of the uniqueness of this Sonship. What I mean is this: One of the strategic, cunning, subtle methods of Satan, to deal with this whole matter to its nullification, is to propagate the doctrine of the universal sonship of mankind. You can hear it on the wireless almost any morning you like. We are all God's sons, if we will look deep enough into our own natures. All we have to do is to turn inward and go deep and we shall find God! Then, by the holy exercises of prayer and the sacraments, we will bring God up out of the depth of our own natures, and bringing Him up, we shall have fellowship with Him! That is the stuff that is preached worldwide today. It is a clever move of the Devil's to get rid of this unique element in sonship, that it is something peculiar, particular, unique. There is no Divine continuity in man. That has been severed, and only by a miracle can union with God be recovered. But Satan, you see, by his false doctrine, and doctrine of demons, has sought to subvert the truth. Is it not of that that Paul says to Timothy, "...in later times some shall fall away from *the faith*, giving heed to seducing spirits and doctrines of demons" (1 Tim. 4:1)? Of course, on the face of it, that sounds terrible: they must surely be very terrible doctrines. No, they are very lovely doctrines! One of them is this doctrine that you have God in you by nature and, if only you will turn into your own heart, you will find God and you can bring Him up by holy exercises, and, if you will but habituate yourself to this practice, you yourself will become Divine. A lovely doctrine, swallowed by the multitude, but a doctrine of demons! It is the Satanic move to get rid of this unique nature of sonship, because that is something apart in God's universe. Satan cannot touch that; it is something outside of his realm, it is unique. "If thou be the Son...". "The Son" and "the faith" represent something exclusive. In refuting one error I am not going to fall into another. Even by being born anew we are not made sons of God in the sense that Christ was the "only begotten" of the Father. We do not partake of deity, but we are made children of God in a sense that is not true of men generally by nature.

In this challenge - "If thou be the Son..." - there is not only recognition of the uniqueness of sonship, but there is the realisation that in that sonship there is a challenge. There is not much challenge to Satan in this other doctrine of the continuity of the Divine in man! But in this sonship of Christ, and of those who are begotten of God, in whom, as Paul says to the Galatians, the Spirit of His Son is ("God sent forth the Spirit of his Son into our hearts" Gal. 4:6), there is a tremendous challenge to Satan, and that is why Satan assailed in this way, and does assail. He would seek in some way to neutralize the spiritual reality of sonship, because it is such a challenge and threatening menace to him and his kingdom.

Paul makes it perfectly clear in Romans 8 that, when the time comes that the sons of God are manifested, then the curse will forever be nullified; that is, all the work of Satan will be destroyed with the manifestation of the sons of God.

The Nature of the Challenge —
Destiny Bound up with Sonship

Well, there is a challenge in sonship, because in that sonship there is all that is included in the destiny of Satan and the destiny of Christ. Satan's destiny is a dark and terrible one: Christ's destiny and the destiny of His own is a glorious one. But these two destinies are not just automatic, they are spiritual. Sonship is something which means a full attainment to a certain relationship and a certain nature.

It is very interesting to note the different usages in the New Testament between the word "child" and "son"; child being one born, son being the child a grown up, coming to maturity. The son, meaning a full-grown one, is sometimes used in this very connection of which we have spoken; meaning that those given to doing evil have come to full growth in it; and you will see that is exactly what happened with the Jews and with Israel in the days of the Lord Jesus. I do not want to become too detailed, but I just indicate it. When the Lord Jesus was speaking to the rulers and the heads of the Jewish nation who were so opposed to Him, He did not speak to them as being children of the Devil, but called them sons. He used the word about them which meant that they were something more than just offspring. They had come to a far measure of maturity in their devilish relationship and work, and when that sonship came to fulness, then Israel is dealt with, judged and cut off.

In the same way, when born from above, we become children of God, and are sons potentially, and when sonship in relation to God has come to full maturity, then the issue is glory, full deliverance. The whole situation is changed with sonship.

Now Satan and his kingdom are coming to that place where the final judgment rests upon the final development of his iniquity. It is sonship in principle. The Old Testament description that answers to it is 'the cup of iniquity being full.' That is only another simile. It is coming to fulness. Sonship, on the side of evil and iniquity, means iniquity full-grown, over-flowing, mature - destruction.

On the other hand, sonship in relation to the Lord, being brought to maturity, means the hour of the Church's maturity, Christ coming to fulness in the saints - "till we all attain unto the unity of the faith... unto a full-grown man" (Eph. 4:13); Christ coming to maturity in His saints. And then what? Well, just the opposite of the destiny of Satan. That is destruction, and this is glory.

The two destinies are bound up, let me repeat, not with some mechanical thing, but with a spiritual nature and development called sonship, and Satan recognises the destiny of sonship, and that is why he challenges it. "If thou be the Son..."

So, the heart and the essence of the faith is the significance of sonship. When again you hear or think of "the faith", always remember in the first place that "the faith" is what Jesus Christ is in the uniqueness of sonship; and, so far as we are concerned, "the faith" is what we are in Him in the uniqueness of sonship. I am not touching upon His deity. Do not misunderstand me in that. That is a sonship of His in which we have no part, in so far as that sonship means deity, but the relationship with God in terms of sonship is shared by us with Him. He is the Heir. "God... hath at the end of these days spoken unto us in his Son, whom he appointed heir of all things" (Heb. 1:2). And then, we are "heirs of God, and joint heirs with Christ" (Rom. 8:17). The principle of sonship is the heart and essence of the faith.

We will leave it there for the time being. But I can say once more that it is in this that the born-anew ones are unique in God's universe, this is what separates them from all others, and with which so great a destiny is bound up. It is upon this that all the conflict rests, and around it all the battle rages. It is because of this we suffer. Do you want less conflict? You can have it at the expense and the meaning of your sonship. If you will not go right on to full growth, you can have a very much easier time, but if you are going right on, you may have the worst time. You are going to know more than any others what spiritual conflict is. You cannot get out of it. Demas evidently found things too hard. "Demas hath forsaken me, having loved this present world" (2 Tim. 4:10). Well, Demas goes back, but those who go on do so by having to accept what Demas found himself unable to accept - an intensifying conflict.

It is not a very comfortable message, but there are the facts. But let us remind ourselves that, if we suffer with Him, we shall reign together with Him (2 Tim. 2:12).

Chapter 2

THE NATURE OF SONSHIP

"When the Son of man cometh, shall he find the faith on the earth?" (Luke 18:8).

Place that passage alongside of those read in our previous meditation (1 Tim. 6:12; 2 Tim. 4:7; Jude 3; Rev. 2:13); we will not repeat them in full just now. Just be reminded that the two passages in Paul's two letters to Timothy were amongst them; first, his exhortation to Timothy to fight the good fight of the faith, and then his own statement that he had fought the good fight and had kept the faith; and we were and are occupied with this phrase - "the faith".

I am quite sure that, in the light of what we said in our previous meditation, the passage in Luke 18:8 takes on new significance and we are better able to understand it. "When the Son of man cometh, shall he find the faith on the earth?" That certainly does not mean, shall He find a Christian system of doctrine on the earth. He will find plenty of that. And it certainly does not mean, shall He find faith in the sense of people who believe in Christianity or in general in Christ. There would be no point, I think in asking that question, if He meant that. There are multitudes of people who believe in a general way in Christ and Christianity, if that could be said to be the meaning of faith, and I do not know that we are to expect that kind of Christianity to diminish very greatly, at least to such a point where it is really a question whether He will find any of it at all when He comes.

But when we look into this phrase, "the faith" as we were doing earlier, and really understand its essence and nature, then the question has some point, and it is really concerning the point of the question that we are going to spend a little time now.

We have sought to see that the faith in its essence is the essential and the unique nature of Divine sonship. It is over that that the fight goes on, rages and intensifies, and that sonship is something into which believers are initially brought by new birth, and thereafter progressively by a life in the Spirit, and it is therefore saying that sonship, in the New Testament sense, is something more than being born into a family; it is growing up in that family, and carries with it the feature of spiritual maturity. A phrase used so frequently in our New Testament is "perfection"; "go on unto perfection" (Heb. 6:1), or as the margin expresses it, "go on to full growth". Really it means the consummation of things, coming to the full end for which you exist.

Seeing then, that that is sonship - going right on to the full end for which you exist as children of God; which, again, implies a life in the Spirit continually - then you have room for the question, shall He find the faith on the earth? In other words, shall He find on the earth a real going on in the Spirit unto full growth? I do not think the question was meant to suggest that He would not find it, that it would not exist at His coming, but I do think that the question contains this factor, namely, that it would be far from being a general thing and that you would have to look for it. In order to find it, you would have to look for it; it will not be there in such a way that everybody can see it. That, I think, is the point of the question.

Well then, we want to look a little more closely at this matter of sonship, seeing that everything is bound up with it. It is the faith, it is the occasion of the conflict, it is the cause of the question of the Lord. What is the nature of sonship? We can answer that by two or three quite simple statements.

Sonship — Essentially and Exclusively of God

Firstly, it is essentially and exclusively of God. We are familiar with the statement in John 1:13: "who were born, not of blood, nor of the will of the flesh, nor of the will of man, but of God". Not this, nor that, nor that, but of God! You might very well put in there - 'but exclusively of God'. Sonship, therefore, is something exclusively of God. It lies altogether beyond the power and possibility of man to achieve, to attain, to reach unto it. It is not in man to produce it or arrive at it. The secret of sonship is not resident in man. The seed of sonship is not in man by nature, in spite of all that of which we spoke in our previous meditation that is the generally accepted doctrine concerning man today. The fact is that this sonship is something which belongs to another realm altogether.

We know that the Word of God sees man as dead, so far as God is concerned, and nothing short of a miracle can change that situation, for life is God's prerogative and gift alone, and resurrection something which is alone in the power of God. Therefore the principle, the law, of sonship is an experience of resurrection which, to those who have it, is such an experience as to settle forever in their convictions that everything they have in relation to God is a sheer miracle of God's own working.

Now, God is going to be very true to that principle and position, and we will discover that a life in the Spirit, which is the life of sonship, cannot be a life in the flesh, cannot be a life out of nature and nature's springs. A life in the Spirit, which is the life of sonship, has continuously behind it the realisation that we cannot live save out from God, that we draw our very life from Him every day. The more we go on with God, which means the more we live in the Spirit, and the more spiritual growth and maturity takes place in us, the deeper will be our consciousness of utter dependence upon God for our life, and for everything in the realm of our relationship with Him. Self-resource, self-strength, self-confidence, self-ability, self-wisdom, self-esteem, self-reputation, will be steadily undermined and sapped and drained by the Spirit of God, and we shall come more and more to the place where we know that it is not in us to be Christians, not in us to live a life in the Spirit, not in us to go on with God. It must all come right out from Himself. Sonship is the most dependent thing of which you can have any conception. He said of Himself, in words perhaps all too familiar to us; "The Son can do nothing out from himself" (John 5:19). Again, "I can of myself do nothing... because I seek not mine own will, but the will of him that sent me". (John 5:30). The Apostle, in the spirit of a true son, will say, "I know nothing by myself..." (1 Cor. 4:4). "We have this treasure in vessels of fragile clay, that the exceeding greatness of the power may be of God, and not of ourselves" (2 Cor. 4:7). "Who is sufficient for these things? ...our sufficiency is of God" (2

Cor. 2:16, 3:5). Now, that is sonship, and that means living continually on the ground of resurrection.

Sonship — Based on Resurrection

And so we come to Romans 1:4: "...declared to be the Son of God in power... by the resurrection of the dead" - sonship based upon resurrection. That is wholly of God, only of God. The Lord Jesus, in putting the truth of sonship into operation, said and did several things which are full of significance in the light of what we are saying. You remember in those early chapters in John how He said, "The hour cometh, when the dead shall hear the *voice of the Son*... and... shall live" (John 5:25). Why? "As the Father raiseth the dead, and giveth them life, even so the Son also giveth life to whom he will" (John 5:21. A.R.V.). This relationship with God in terms of sonship means that by dependence upon God, by a life in God, a life in the Spirit, that which is God's sole and exclusive prerogative of raising the dead becomes an actual fact in the sphere of sonship, an actuality at work in the sphere of sonship. The Son becomes the sphere in which the Father's power and right of resurrection operates. But, while that is true, that resurrection life is working through the Son from the Father, the Son is still saying in the very same parts of the Word, "The Son can do nothing out from himself, but what he seeth the Father doing" (John 5:19). That is in the early part of John.

You get well on in John and you have the case of Lazarus, and Lazarus is taken up, as you know by the introduction to the incident, with one object. The Lord Jesus states the object of Lazarus' sickness and death. "This sickness is not unto death, but for the glory of God, that the *Son* of God may be glorified" (John 11:4). And so Lazarus is not healed. The Lord Jesus does not come to the home in Bethany as the doctor to give a remedy, and to recover Lazarus. He stays away deliberately until Lazarus is not only beyond hope in this life, but is beyond this life itself, and then, when the Lord Jesus knows that he is dead, He says, "Our friend Lazarus sleepeth". The disciples misunderstood and thought He meant that he was having a sleep: so Jesus said plainly, "Lazarus is dead". Then, when He knew in His spirit that Lazarus was gone, He came to Bethany. He was acting out now what He had said before, and the thing which governs the action is "that the Son may be glorified". Then John sums up the whole of that Gospel in the words of chapter 20:31: "These things are written that ye may believe that Jesus is the Christ, the Son of God". The whole of John's Gospel is written with that object in view.

Now John has written the statement which we have about the Son raising the dead by His relationship and life in the Father, and dependence upon the Father, and John too has written about Lazarus; and he says, I have written all these things and all the other things with one point in view, namely, "that ye may believe that Jesus is the Christ, the Son of God". Sonship is all the time on this basis of resurrection.

What was true in the case of the Lord Jesus is true of the spirit of sonship, wherever that spirit is found. Turning to Galatians again, the Apostle says, "Because ye are sons, God sent forth the Spirit of his Son into our hearts, crying, Abba, Father" (Gal. 4:6). We are sons. But how many of the Lord's people are willing to live on that basis? How many there are who want to have it in themselves; the strength, the wisdom, the ability, the efficiency; everything in themselves, not a life of utter dependence and daily resurrection. "When the Son of man cometh, shall he, find the faith...."? You see the point - something which is exclusively of God; *and God takes pains to undercut every tendency and inclination to have it in ourselves,* because that is the way in which at the first this very purpose of God in sonship was set aside.

The Law of Faith and Dependence

Adam was created with sonship in view, sonship after this kind, but he was placed upon the basis of dependence upon God, faith and dependence. That was the law of his life, and that was to be the law by which he would come to the realisation of sonship in its full sense. Satan came and suggested to Adam that he could have it in himself if he liked. He need not have it of God and have to look to God all the time. If Adam did but follow his advice, there need be none of this servitude to God, but he could be as God and have it in himself, and be delivered from the bondage of this life of dependence and faith, and obedience. Adam accepted that suggestion and sought to take it, to have it in himself without reference or deference to God. Sonship was lost for Adam and his race. The last Adam comes and accepts a life of absolute dependence upon the Father, and obedience to the Father in an utter self-emptying. "He emptied himself... and became obedient"; He took "the form of a bond-servant" (Phil. 2:6-8). He had it not in Himself, by His own choice: He had it in the Father; and sonship was established, realised and expressed in fulness in Him.

We, beloved, are called on to that basis. Oh, there is nothing which will work against the spirit of sonship, God's purpose of fulness in us, like pride, the pride which wants to have it in ourselves. Pride hates a life of dependence. Pride cannot bear to have to look outside of itself for everything. Pride must have the root of things in itself. "Be not wise in your own conceits" is a phrase the Apostle used (Rom. 12:16). What is conceit? The very word itself means "having the seat of things in yourself"; wise by having the seat of things in yourself. The Lord Jesus, Who had the highest place in heavenly glory, the highest and greatest title and name - all rights were in His power - accepted the position of girding Himself with a towel and putting water into a basin and kneeling down to wash the feet of His disciples. That is the mind which was in Christ Jesus. That is sonship. It is not nice for the flesh, nor for our reputation, it is not pleasant to our education; we look for something better than that. But that is sonship. That is a life in the Spirit. That spirit will be the mark, the hall-mark, of spiritual growth, of spiritual maturity. The person who is really growing spiritually is not the person who is becoming something important spiritually. The one who is growing is the one who is growing in the servant dependent spirit more and more. The one who can get down lowest is the one who is really getting up highest.

That is the nature of sonship. It is something which is wholly of God, exclusively of God, not of ourselves. We cannot produce it.

Sonship — a Spiritual Thing

It is, therefore, in the next place, a spiritual thing. "That which is born of the flesh is flesh; and that which is born of the Spirit is spirit" (John 3:6). Sonship, therefore, is essentially a spiritual thing and is always connected, in the Word, with the Spirit. The new birth is connected with the Spirit - "born of the Spirit". "As many as are led by the Spirit of God, these are sons of God" (Rom. 8:14). Born; led. You come to Galatians: Galatians is just full of these things, full of sonship and the Spirit. "Because ye are sons, God sent forth the Spirit of his Son into our hearts, crying, Abba, Father." Then you know Paul's argument about Hagar and Ishmael, and Sarah and Isaac; the one born after the flesh, the other born after the Spirit; and the one born after the flesh is to be cast out, that the one born after the Spirit may be established (Gal. 4:21-31). It is sonship and the Spirit again. Sonship, therefore, is a spiritual thing. It is obvious that this kind of sonship is not a natural thing.

Sonship — Indestructible in Itself
The Work of Satan to Nullify its Power

But the point that I want to get at and emphasise is this, that because it is a spiritual thing, it is something which interests Satan in a particular way. Being exclusively of God and being wholly spiritual, it is something which, shall I say, tantalises Satan; it is a cause of tremendous annoyance and grievance to him. He cannot get at this thing directly, it is beyond him. You notice that in the Word of God there is no denial from any realm that there is such a being as the Son of God or as the Christ. There is no denial; that is recognised, acknowledged and accepted everywhere. There is a denial that *Jesus* is the Son of God, but the fact of sonship as a reality in God's universe is never questioned. Antichrist is not the denial of the existence of Christ, but the counterfeiting of Christ: and that is a tremendous admission, a tremendous acknowledgment. If you counterfeit something, it is your way of admitting that there is something real. You do not counterfeit if there is not the genuine thing. You see my point. There is something in God's universe which is never questioned or denied, but which is an established thing, which cannot be touched as a reality, and that is sonship. To get at that - well, anything can be done to nullify it in its effect - but the fact is there, and it is that fact which is Satan's aggravation and annoyance, the fact of the existence of this sonship, in God's universe, and that that sonship has invaded and come into his domain. There is sonship right in the very domain of Satan, in the kingdom of this world, this world which "lieth in the wicked one". Sonship has invaded and come into it; and there is a fact which cannot be destroyed, it is inviolate in itself.

Oh, lay hold of this! Sonship is something which Satan cannot destroy in itself. Sonship, is something inviolate, lying outside of Satan's realm and Satan's power. What then is the nature of the battle? Oh, Satan is not so foolish as to think that he can destroy sonship as a fact, but all his efforts and methods are employed to nullify the effect of it as he can, as he will, in his domain. After this manner, therefore, he started with the last Adam - "If thou be the Son...". The sting is in that "if". If only the Lord Jesus would admit an "if", Satan has scored, and while the sonship is not destroyed, the effect of it in his kingdom is.

That can be put in another way. Admit a doubt, admit a question, and you are undone, and the thing which in itself is inviolate is put under arrest with regard to its effect against Satan. Doubt, unbelief, a question, an uncertainty, suspends the tremendous potency of sonship as against the enemy, even though the sonship position cannot be destroyed. If Satan can find a people here who believe on the basis of sonship, and persist in believing, and refuse to doubt and question, he has found sonship there which corresponds to what he found in Christ, Who said, "The prince of this world cometh and hath nothing in me" (John 14:30). Hath nothing! What is he looking for? The ground of a question or a doubt, is what he is after; and he found nothing.

So the faith you see, is faith which is reposed in God's Son and which makes that sonship a mighty power in the one who believes.

Now, what we are saying is that the existence of this thing called sonship is the occasion of all the conflict because it is something which in itself is beyond Satan's power, and unless in some way its effect in his kingdom is neutralised, it is going to be his ultimate expulsion and undoing. Let us say again that, lying right there at the heart of sonship, is no less a thing than the ridding of this universe of Satan and his kingdom.. That is the issue of sonship. Therefore let us look at the nature of sonship. What is it? It is a life in the Spirit. Satan will constantly try to provoke unto a life in the flesh. A life of dependence: then Satan will try to make us independent. A life of humility, meekness, drawing wholly upon the Lord for everything: then Satan will try to provoke us to pride, to have it in ourselves, to be something ourselves, to care for our reputation, to fight for our own vindication. Remember that every tendency, inclination or attempt to secure our vindication - we may be right, but that is not the question - anything in the direction of securing our vindication is against sonship. "He made himself of no reputation" (Phil. 2:7). He did not seek to vindicate Himself or to be vindicated. He left the matter of vindication altogether with God, and became obedient unto death, yea, the death of the Cross. "Their righteousness is of me, saith the Lord" (Isa. 54:17). Oh, for this grace of self-emptying, seeking no title, no name, no reputation, no vindication, no justification for ourselves. It cuts the ground from under the feet of the enemy, robs him of that which he needs to save his own position and to nullify the effect of Christ's presence. Let us ask the Lord for that grace of selflessness, and of joyful acceptance of a life of dependence upon the Lord in terms of daily resurrection. That is the way of sonship. It makes room for the Lord and for the fulness of Christ.

I think perhaps we could very well close there just now. Do not forget that Satan is out to bring the effect of sonship under arrest in his kingdom. He cannot destroy it, that is something beyond his power, but he can nullify its power so far as his interests are concerned, and he does that by trying to get us to violate the very laws of sonship. Those laws of sonship we have mentioned. They are shown in the life of the Son Himself so clearly - nothing in Himself, but dependence upon the Father, altogether dependent upon the Father. A life in which the law of resurrection is a daily and hourly operation and experience, a life without personal name, reputation, standing or vindication, a life wholly handed over to God, these and many other things comprise sonship, and are the marks of a life in the Spirit.

The Lord make us good sons for His own glory and satisfaction.

29

Chapter 3

THE LIBERTY OF SONS

"Paul, an apostle (not from men, neither through man, but through Jesus Christ, and God the Father, who raised him from the dead)... I make known to you, brethren, as touching the gospel which was preached by me, that it is not after man. For neither did I receive it from man, nor was I taught it, but through revelation of Jesus Christ... it was the good pleasure of God... to reveal his Son in me, that I might preach him among the Gentiles; straightway I conferred not with flesh and blood... but they only heard say, He that once persecuted us now preacheth the faith of which he once made havoc" (Gal. 1:1,11-12,15,23).

In this time together so far, the Lord has directed our attention to that little clause - "the faith." The passages basic to our meditation have been those in the two letters of Paul to Timothy, first his exhortation to Timothy to fight the good fight of the faith, and then his own statement as to himself at the end - "I have fought the good fight, I have kept the faith," and it is into something of the meaning and significance of that phrase, "the faith," that we are being led to inquire at this time.

Here it is again in Gal. 1:23 - "He that once persecuted us now preacheth the faith of which he once made havoc." What was it that Saul of Tarsus sought to destroy, of which he set himself to make havoc? Well, he was a Jew, and of the Jewish party in Jerusalem, who summed up their charge and accusation against the Lord Jesus in those words - "He made himself the Son of God" (John 19:7). As we said before, it was not just the coming in of a new and rival religion, but something very much deeper than that, and all that is contained in that designation "the Son of God" (Jesus, the Son of

God) is what is meant by "the faith." In a word, it is sonship, and all that sonship means as something that is out from God, and which has come into this world, and which being here, is altogether other than that which is already here: different in nature and different in position, and therefore different in destiny; something in this universe which is unique - sonship.

All the forces of hell, and of this world which lieth in the wicked one, are set against that sonship; in Christ primarily, pre-eminently, and then in those who are begotten of God, sons of God, through faith in Jesus Christ. It is that spiritual reality, that spiritual thing, namely, sonship which is the object and occasion of all hostility that makes it necessary for believers to fight. The contention is not for a creed, not for a system of truth, not for fundamentalism, but for a spiritual position and a spiritual nature, and for all that sonship means from God's standpoint; and for all that that sonship means from Satan's standpoint. As we said before, wherever we come on this matter of "the faith," we find ourselves at once in very close proximity to the element of conflict. Wherever it is mentioned, nearby there is warfare.

May I just repeat one word said in our previous meditation when we were thinking about our Lord's words recorded by Luke - "When the Son of man cometh, shall he find the faith on the earth?" (Luke 18:8). The question does not relate to what is called in general "the Christian faith." There will be plenty of the Christian faith on the earth. The Lord Jesus would have been a bad prophet, and have had very little foresight, had His question meant that in the day of His appearing there would be very little Christianity on the earth, in that general sense. No, His question went much deeper than that, and it is a very real question, if we recognise that sonship is something which has to be brought to fulness in believers, something which relates to Christ coming to fulness in His own and of His members coming into His fulness, unto that ultimate manifestation of the sons in full growth. If that is the meaning of sonship, then indeed there is room for the question - "Shall he find the faith on this earth?"

That could be put in other words. Shall He find on the earth a people who are really going right on in sonship to the fulness of Christ? And I do not think there is any doubt about the answer. He will certainly find a great many Christians who are not going right on, who have stopped short. It will not be so easy to find these who will go right on.

My trouble this morning is lack of time, and I really do not know where to begin and what to say, because the whole New Testament gathers around this very thing.

The New Testament as a whole - of course, I am referring to the Epistles - the New Testament as a whole just comes right down on this question of who is going on, or who is going to come under this terrible arresting effort of the enemy, in the matter of spiritual growth.

A Legal System Works Against the Faith

When you come to the letter to the Galatians alone - and I am led there very definitely at this time - you know Paul has hardly got through his introductory word before he says, 'I marvel that you are so soon brought to a standstill, that your going on has so quickly been arrested.' The whole letter is on that matter, namely, their arrest, and Paul's urge that they should throw off the thing which has come upon them to arrest them, and go on.

And what is it that has come in to arrest? Well, it is the same thing you find in so many other directions in the Church of the New Testament times. It is those Judaizers from Jerusalem who were following Paul wherever he went, coming after him and in amongst the fruits of his ministry, his converts, and saying, "Except ye be circumcised, ye cannot be saved," bringing in the old traditional system of religion, a fixed thing, in all its legality, and seeking to impose it upon them. And the tragedy, the shame, the grief of it is this, that it is so infectious that even a Peter can become contaminated; even a Peter, a pillar in the Church, a foremost apostle, a good and godly man, devoted to and serving the Lord. Here in this letter to the Galatians, Paul says, 'Certain came down from James, and Peter was infected, and he compromised, and I withstood him to the face.' That is a terrible passage, a terrible situation. But do you see what it implies? There are few people so good, so high up spiritually, so distinguished for their service to the Lord, and their relationship with the Lord, so few who cannot be infected with this something which works so insidiously against the faith in its essence: good men, godly men, devout men, Peters, men of the first three, touched by this thing that is at work. What is it? A legal system set and fixed, be it Jewish or Christian, which straddles the path of going right on with the Lord to His full thought, which just comes right in the way of all that sonship means.

For you see how the Apostle leads right off on this matter of sonship in the letter to the Galatians. He is dealing with this spiritual, heavenly seed. His introduction is all concerning that. 'Paul, an apostle, not of men but of God, Who raised Jesus from the dead... to deliver us from this present evil world.' How significant is every word. There is something here that is not of this earth, not from down here at all, something not of men - "I received it not of man, I was not taught it of man." There is something here that is from heaven. This thing from heaven was on the basis of resurrection; and that is of God, and God only, something above all that is here. We are delivered from this present evil world or age, and Paul in his mind was not only thinking of the vast, sinful world of paganism and heathenism; he was thinking also of the religious world. "It pleased God to reveal his Son in me." We mark, then, all the spiritual elements about his very introductory words.

Where the Fight of the Faith Arises

And then, when he has struck tremendous blows at this system of things, this religious system, and has challenged Peter over it, in respect of his dissimulation, he goes on about this heavenly and spiritual seed. "We are sons of God by faith in Jesus Christ" (Gal. 3:26). Then he moves to Ishmael and Isaac, the seed after the flesh and the seed after the Spirit, and brings in this whole matter of what sonship really is, as being something after the Spirit. What he is saying in this whole letter is just this in a word: Sonship, with all that God means by sonship, is what is in view, and over against it there is this breaking in continually of things religious, subtle, beautiful, with all the argument that God is in them; but, nevertheless, breaking in with one object, all hidden from sight, namely, to cut right across the path of the believer in his going right on to God's fullest thought in sonship; and it sets up a warfare.

Let us be perfectly frank and plain. Beloved, it is true that there are many good people, many leading Evangelical people, many Peters if you like, touching whose devotion to the Lord we can have no question: their zeal, their consecration, is not open to discussion; and yet they are so tied by a fixed system that they become points of conflict where the matter of going right on with the Lord is concerned. They oppose, they make the difficulty and the trouble: and it is not themselves personally but the thing which binds them. In principle it is this Judaism cropping up again, a fixed system which has held for generations and centuries, a tradition which is established, and anything that seems to require a superseding of that tradition - I choose the word carefully - at once provokes antagonism and conflict. Is it not strange? Why do I use the word supersede? Because of what Paul says here. He says there are those who have come in with another Gospel, which is not another. He means this, that all that came in with Israel was intended to lead right on to Christ, but now it is being used to hold back from Christ. The effect of it is to obstruct the way of realising the end for which it exists. It is not really two things that are here. Christ is the complement and the fulfilment of all that came in through Moses, and if only you understand and interpret Moses aright, you will go right on with Christ. But now this thing is brought in as though it were another thing. Really, in essence the two things are one, intended to be one, in the thought of God, but it is being made two things now. But the intention of God is that there should be this glorious issue - Christ in fulness: so that, what can lead to Christ is to be superseded by Christ. You are not going to say that Judaism is all wrong, you are not going to say, all the Old Testament is wrong, is false, you are not going to say that what came in through Moses is all error. Not at all! But you are going to say that it was intended to come to a place where all that to which it was pointing would supersede it.

Oh, the conflict is there, and the fight of the faith comes right in amongst Paul and Peter in principle. That is a terrible thing. The fight of the faith! Oh, you would never find Paul and Peter fighting one another over the deity of Christ. You would never find them in conflict over any of these fundamentals of Christianity; the inspiration of the Scriptures, the Person of the Lord Jesus, the coming again. Oh no. You would find them absolutely one on all those matters, however many they were. But here, strangely, we find Peter and Paul in conflict, one having to withstand the other to the face, and it is the faith which is involved.

What the Faith Is

What is the faith? The faith is this, that Jesus is the Son of God. But that is something more than a personal, objective relationship. That is a spiritual reality which has to come into expression through Him in the Church, in His members as representing the heavenly seed, coming to the fulness of Christ; which being accomplished, is to supplant and oust all this other seed which Satan has introduced into God's universe. That is the faith. The faith comes down to this, namely, what we are spiritually in God's universe. That is the faith.

What are we intended to be? We are intended to be in our experience, in our spiritual life, in our presence here, a living proof that Jesus is the Son of God; not just to declare this as a tenet of our faith and creed, but to be here as children of God growing up into sonship, by which sonship His sonship is put into expression. Do you follow what I mean?

Oh, it is over this that there is all the conflict, and I say again, the conflict gets right in inside, amongst godly people, godly men, devout men. Why? Because some are so held by their traditions, by their fixed system, by the thing established here in Christianity. Somehow or other that very thing gets in the way of what Paul calls here in the Galatian letter "the liberty of sons."

The Liberty of Sons

I wonder what that phrase means to you, what it is becoming to mean to you - the liberty of sons. Oh, if you have known bondage to legal Christianity and the Lord has led you in any measure into spiritual liberty, that is a very cherished phrase - the liberty of sons. It is a great, great position to be in. You are not being brow-beaten in your conscience for a moment about what you must do or must not do, this whole tremendous, colossal system of Shalts and Shalt nots that has come into the midst of Christianity, making Christianity into something that is put on you. They bind heavy burdens and grievous to be borne, and lay them on men's shoulders (Matt. 23:4). That is what the Lord said about the Jews, but that is what many Christians are doing, and it is very easy for us to slip into the position where our Christianity and the Christian life becomes a burden almost grievous to be borne.

To be emancipated from that into the liberty of sons; what does this mean, and how is it brought about? You go after the Lord, that is all. It is not a thing, a system, it is Himself, Christ. Skim through this Galatian letter and put your pencil mark under every mention of the name of Christ, and you will get a surprise; and you have got the message of the letter, for it all resolves itself into this - it is the Lord, not Judaism, not Christianity, not a system at all; it is the Lord. And if it is the Lord, you are emancipated; you need not worry about anything else. You will not go wrong on any of those thousand points, if it is the Lord upon Whom you are set. You are bound to go right, if you are after the Lord. That is liberty, and that is deliverance.

You see the nature of the conflict. The fight of the faith is not fighting with modernism in the first instance, nor standing for the virtues of the Christian faith. It may work out that way, it may at times have to do with that, and doubtless it does include that, but there is something very much deeper than that. Right in the innermost part of our being we know there is a spiritual conflict going on, and that spiritual conflict has to do with whether we are going on with the Lord, and that going on with the Lord is the development or outworking of sonship, it is coming to the consummation of sonship. That is where the challenge is, and anything the enemy can bring in to stop that, he will.

The Lord give us light on all this.

Chapter 4

REVELATION IN RELATION TO SONSHIP

"Paul, an apostle (not from men, neither through man, but through Jesus Christ, and God the Father, who raised him from the dead)... I make known to you, brethren, as touching the gospel, which was preached by me, that it is not after man. For neither did I receive it from man, nor was I taught it, but through revelation of Jesus Christ... it was the good pleasure of God... to reveal his Son in me... I conferred not with flesh and blood: neither went I up to Jerusalem to them that were apostles before me: but I went away into Arabia; and again I returned unto Damascus... they only heard say, He that once persecuted us now preacheth the faith of which he once made havoc" (Gal. 1:1,11-12,15-17,23-24).

I want to seek, as the Lord enables us, to get still closer to this matter of sonship, and I think there is no doubt that Paul, as he comes before us in this letter to the Galatians, himself stands as an example of what sonship is. There is no doubt that much of the nature of sonship is resident in these statements of his about himself - "not from men, neither through a man, but through Jesus Christ, and God the Father, who raised him from the dead", and other passages which are similar.

"An Apostle, not after Men"

The question arises - and it is a very simple way I think, of getting to understand what is indicated - the question arises, How might Paul have been an apostle other than by this method, other than in this way - "an apostle not from men, neither through a man: the Gospel which I preach not after man, neither did I receive it from a man, nor was I taught it". What did he mean? Well, there were two ways in which Paul could have become an apostle and a preacher of the Gospel. There were the apostles at Jerusalem with whom he went up later, and if he had been an interested inquirer, he might have gone perhaps to one of their meetings, or might have called upon them for an interview, and they, Peter, James and John, and others, might have told him all that they knew about Jesus, and have given him a good deal of what they had heard him say through the three years, and also of the many and mighty miracles which He wrought; and then about His death; and then with tremendous earnestness, passion, zeal and fire and enthusiasm, of His resurrection. Thus they might have given Saul all those facts, and given them in such a way, with such fire and such earnestness as to be tremendously persuasive. The young man might have fallen to that because the thing seemed to be indisputable, so real, so wonderful to them. He might say, There is no doubt that these men have seen something, and they know something, and what they say is true! Then, as a result of it all, he might have said, Well, what can I do but accept what they say, believe that they are speaking the truth, and myself just become a follower of Jesus Christ and, accepting these facts and believing them, go out and declare them to other people? He might have become an apostle in that way. That is what he meant when he said, "of men", "through a man". It might have been like that. It could have been like that, and it has been like that in multitudes of cases; not just the acceptance of the argument, but the contagion of someone else's belief, becoming enthused by the others.

It is not a question of whether they were right, or whether what they said was the truth. That is not the point at all. Nor is it in question whether their experience was a true one. There is no doubt at all regarding the truth and reality of their experience. Yet other people may have an experience, and be in a perfectly true and right position; it may be the most living and real thing with them; and their zeal and their passion and their conviction, and all that they know, the truth which they possess, may be given to you, may be passed on to you, and you may accept it quite honestly and sincerely, and in a sense you may believe it, and in that way go on with the Lord Jesus and become a Christian and a servant of Christ: and it is just between that and something else which, after all, is altogether different, that this whole matter of sonship arises.

The Need for a Revelation of Christ in the Heart

Paul says, "It pleased God... to reveal his Son in me". It pleased God likewise to reveal His Son in Peter, and in James and in John. Yes, but that is not good enough for me, and, while I may not question or doubt their experience or their knowledge, or the facts which they state, sonship in my case demands that God shall reveal his Son in me, and that I do not get it even from those who are reputed to be something, pillars in the Church, Peter, James or John. "It pleased God... to reveal his Son in me." I received it not from men, be they the twelve Apostles; neither through a man, be he Peter, but through revelation of Jesus Christ.

That is very simple and elementary, but it sets forth the difference; and that is what Paul is drawing attention to. He does not, in so many words, say, Now, this is what sonship is, it is a revelation of God's Son in the heart of a person. He does not put it quite precisely like that, but that is what this letter stands for, and that is what the New Testament makes perfectly clear as being the real nature of sonship. It is that this whole matter of the Lord Jesus has become a personal and, in a right and proper sense, an independent thing in our own hearts. Our testimony must be, not, I was brought up in a Christian home, and sent to Sunday School and taken to church, and instructed in these things of the Lord, and given a sound Bible teaching; not that - that may all be receiving it through or of men, or a man. There has to be something more than that. We have to be able to say, "God that said, Light shall shine out of darkness, hath shined into our hearts, to give the light of the knowledge of the glory of God in the face of Jesus Christ" (2 Cor. 4:6).

"In our hearts" - that is where sonship begins, and it is that which is sonship from beginning to end; an initial thing where we leap clear of everything that is second-hand and the thing becomes first-hand, and where it grows and grows and never stops growing as a first-hand thing. That is sonship. If you understand and can grasp what that means, then you know what sonship is.

You see, about every fresh case of revelation there is a sense in which everything is quite new, as though the thing revealed had never been before, and no one else in all God's universe had ever heard or seen it. When you really come to have that experience, that knowledge by revelation of the Lord Jesus may be very imperfect, it may be only one thing about Him, but it is the revelation of the Lord Jesus in some particular way, at some particular point, some particular significance; and when you come in this way of revelation into possession of that it is to you as though it is something that has just come out of heaven newborn, and no one else in all the world has ever had it before. That is the effect of it. You want to tell it to other people, and old stagers who have known it for years and years have become your pupils. You begin to teach them something they know about as though they knew nothing of it at all. That is the effect of it. Of course, they do not let on; they do not smile benignly, and say, Poor creature! Inwardly they may smile, but it is a smile of gratification. They know that is how it ought to be with you. But they know quite well exactly what has happened. It is just like that. Some of us know that, when we did, by the grace of God and the operation of the Holy Spirit, leap clear of all that we had known in that other way, that traditional way, into the knowledge of the same thing in a living way by revelation, then we began to talk about it, and it did not matter to us at all that there had been people saying the same thing for years, or that it could be found in a good many books. To us it was as though they knew nothing about it at all. We were the only ones who knew anything about it! That is quite pardonable. If it really is of the first-hand order, there is something which is quite new and quite fresh, as though it had just come for the first time out of heaven. That is sonship.

Oh, if we lived there right up to date all the time, how different things would be. I mean, how much of our knowledge is, after all, what we have got through men, or of a man. And Paul is saying, Now, I could have got it all from the elders and apostles at Jerusalem and become a good Christian and an apostle, a servant of

Jesus Christ like that. But no - "Paul an apostle (not from men, neither through a man, but through Jesus Christ, and God the Father, who raised him from the dead)."

Revelation Makes for Stability

Now we want to see how this connects with the whole object of the letter to the Galatians. These Galatians had, as the apostle said, started well, and for a little while they had run well, and then they had stopped because the traditionalists, the Judaizers, had come in and bewitched them, and their going on had been arrested; they had proved unstable. "I marvel", says the Apostle, "that you are so quickly removing from him that called you in the grace of Christ unto another gospel" (Gal. 1:6). I marvel! "O foolish Galatians, who did bewitch you... having begun in the Spirit, are ye now perfected in the flesh?" (Gal. 3:1,3). They had proved to be fickle, unstable, unreliable: and such features are not the features of sonship. They are just the opposite; they are the contradiction of sonship.

Now what is implied, if it is not directly stated, by the Holy Spirit through the Apostle is this, that when it is after this kind - "God revealed his Son in me" - when it is first-hand, immediate, direct, personal, the revelation of God's Son in us, it makes for stability, it makes for assurance, it rules out all fickleness. Immediately you get on to second-hand ground, you get on to dangerous ground, so far as your stability is concerned. Presently a storm will arise, the rains will come, the winds will blow and beat upon that house, and it will fall: and great will be the fall of it, because it was built upon the sand. You remember what our Lord said: "He that heareth these sayings of mine, and doeth them not, shall be likened unto a foolish man, which built his house upon the sand". It implies something that is not rooted in experience, not rooted in ourselves, something we have heard and that is as far as it got. We have got it second-hand. The Galatians met the adverse winds and rains of the Judaizing assaults and crashed. Paul then, says, by implication, stability, assurance, trustworthiness in the spiritual life, demand that we shall have this first-hand knowledge by revelation of the Lord; and if it is a demand, it is a possibility, it is meant for us; and it is just that freshness of things by first-hand knowledge and revelation which brings the element of wonderful freshness and life into every case concerned.

There is all the difference, you see, between that Christian life which is a labouring under the burden of an imposed Christian order and system, requirement and demand, and the free life of a son in whom the joy of the Lord is the strength. I cannot help asking this question of you, Is your Christian life a burden? Are you under a strain because you belong to the Lord? Have you come into a realm - you may use phraseology and call it "the testimony" or something of the kind - into a realm which has brought you into a strain and you ever wear a look of strain on your face, and go about as though you were carrying a great burden: this testimony is something so exacting and you have to be so careful? Has your Christian life become anything like that, a strenuous burdensome thing which takes the real joy out of your life, and people feel that you are all the time trying to live up to something, to keep up a standard, to maintain something? That is all wrong, every bit of it is wrong. That is not sonship; that is slavery. That is what Galatians deals with, the great difference between the son and the slave. Sonship carries with it in the heart always the sense of wonder, of freshness of life. It does not mean you have no burdens and trials, but it does mean that your relationship to the Lord is a thing which is so real, so first-hand, and your knowledge of the Lord is so fresh, that you know that you are on the borders of a land of far distances. You know in your own heart what these words mean - "Thine eyes shall see the king in his beauty: they shall behold the land of far distances" (Isa. 33:17). I am not exaggerating and I am not straining to make this mean something. To some of us it is just like that. For us we know that we have come to the land of far distances. That can be put in other words. We are seeing so much, sensing so much, that we realise quite well we will never get through it, and never be able to give it out or even to exhaust it, though we were to go on here for many a lifetime. It is like that.

Is it like that with you, or are you living on the last crumb, hardly knowing how to make ends meet spiritually? It is the difference in sonship, you see. Sonship implies an open heaven, sonship does bring in this element of wonder. Oh, friends, it is very true; and I would not say that to you if it were not true in my own case. I know this tremendous difference. Life is cut in two for some of us. On the one side of life, there was that strain to get something, to meet the demand, working hard to get some fresh idea, buying the latest books in order to try and keep fresh in our preaching, getting new ideas. People who were the most suggestive or provocative of thought and idea were our favourite authors. Then came the dividing of life with death and resurrection, with the Cross, and the other half of life, the growing revelation of the Lord Jesus that, no matter how long you go on, you feel that you have not started, but are still right at the beginning. It is a wonderful thing to feel you have the land of far distances, and are seeing the King in His beauty. That is the inheritance of sons. Christ is the land of far distances, He is the King in His beauty; and the land is our inheritance; we are brought into the land. It is a wonderful land.

Revelation Leads to Loneliness

Yes, that is quite true, that is all true, and yet there is something else about sonship which is equally true though not perhaps so happy. This revelation of Christ in us, when it is a true, real, living revelation, not only leads to and makes for stability and assurance and confidence, wonder and freshness and life, but it leads to loneliness, and I should be false to you if I did not say so, and indicate what that means; because the majority even of Christians are still hide-bound by tradition. They are still all of that other kind: what they have received they have received through men or from a man; they have taken on an already completed, rounded-off system of truth and teaching called Christianity. They have entered into it and taken it up, and they cannot see beyond it. You do not question their sincerity, nor do you doubt their earnestness, but there is that about all they have which is so second-hand. It is something which has existed through the Christian centuries, developed by this one and that one, shaped, formed and phrased by different teachers. It has become the evangel, evangelical Christianity in all its set terms, phraseology and forms. They do not see beyond it. And when one moves out of that realm into a personal, direct knowledge of the

Lord through what we often term an open heaven, - but not, mark you, through a new or different revelation of Christ that is something apart from the Scriptures - into that experience, where we can say, "It pleased God to reveal his Son in me, and with me it is so real that sometimes I wonder if anyone has such a knowledge, such an experience"; when we move that way, we move into a lonely realm. The majority cannot follow, cannot go with us, and cannot understand.

It does seem to me that there was something of that about Paul, that even other apostles were not able to grasp or apprehend Paul. He seemed to be very much one by himself. Yet here too we see the wonderful grace of God. Regarding what I said to you in our previous meditation about Paul and Peter having to have it out, and Paul resisting Peter to his face, I think I ought to add a word which improves on that situation. It is quite true Paul had a very straight talk with Peter. That is putting it mildly, I think. The words are strong words - "I resisted him to his face". But I think it is a great thing that years after when Peter wrote his letter he writes of him as, "Our beloved brother Paul" (2 Pet. 3:15). It is all right. It shows the grace of God; the final offence has not been taken, fellowship has not been broken. "Our beloved brother Paul." Peter coming back after being resisted to his face. Well, we just add that word and leave it.

But, you see, it does seem that even Paul, surrounded though he was by all the other apostles, had to go a lonely way, because this revelation was to him something so personal. It does mean that: understand that; and probably some of you do understand it in your experience. It will put you very largely into a lonely position, so far as the majority of other Christians are concerned, if you are going this way.

A Word of Warning —
What is Meant when we Speak of Revelation

But I will step back a little, to safeguard and cover something. You have to be very careful about this matter of revelation, and I am not thinking for one moment of a revelation which is a different and a fresh revelation of the Lord Jesus from that given to the Lord's people in our own time or in other times. I am only speaking of it coming to us as revelation. Let us be very careful that we do not give the impression that we think that we are constituted by a special revelation which none of the Lord's people elsewhere have had or have. That is not the case, nor is that our idea at all. What we do seek to stand and live for is that the full revelation of the Lord Jesus shall come in our case in such a living way as to remove us altogether from merely traditional ground, and put us on to living ground. That is what it means, that the thing is living.

It is a difference, beloved, in another sense, in the sense that the Lord has done something by which it has been possible for Him to make His truth living in a fuller way than is true of that which is merely a traditional and set system, and an old order of things. That is the difference here in the letter to the Galatians. What Peter, James and John and all the others had was perfectly right, and Paul was not in any way different from them in any fundamental matter, or in the manner of his knowing, though in the measure of revelation he may have far outstripped others. But the point is, that whatever the other apostles may have had, and whatever Paul may have learnt from them, all that had to come to him likewise by revelation; he had not just to receive it second-hand. That is the difference; and it is that which makes for these things of which I have spoken, and it is that which makes for real helpfulness and power. We are not really helped by second-hand truth, second-hand revelation. It may be a very fine address, the substance of it may be perfectly true, and we may see that the person who gives it really knows it; but oh, then there is the gap! What do we need? Not just to adopt it because they see it and believe it, and because it is true in their case, but it has to be made as true in our case. And when it becomes like that, true sonship in that sense, then we are in a position to be really helpful to others; for, while we cannot give them our experience, we can help them very much to see that there is such an experience, and that it is for them.

First-hand Experience Alone Makes a Servant of God

I have just said, in very simple language, another thing which is very far reaching and compasses a great deal of ground in the Word of God. Real service does not come by being "trained". We are never made servants of God by going to Bible Institutes. They may be good things, very helpful, very useful, but they do not make a servant of God. You cannot be trained to be a servant of God in this academic sense. "It pleased God... to reveal his Son in me, that I might preach him among the Gentiles." It pleased God to send me to College, that I might preach Him? No, it pleased God to reveal His Son in me, that I might preach Him. Real service of the Lord comes out of that sonship. In the Word of God, sonship always lies behind service - The Levites and priests, sons of Aaron; service, sonship.

The Testing and Perfecting of Sonship in the Wilderness

Now, Paul says, "When it pleased God... to reveal his Son in me... immediately I conferred not with flesh and blood: neither went I up to Jerusalem to them that were apostles before me; but I went away into Arabia". It seems to me that what Arabia stands for is always very closely related with sonship. Moses had forty years of it. Well, he was truly far more a son when he came out than when he went in, in a spiritual sense.

"The heavens were opened... and a voice... said, Thou art my beloved Son; in thee I am well pleased... Then was Jesus led of the Spirit into the wilderness" (Luke 3:21-22; 4:1). Sonship was being dealt with there. "If thou be the Son...." That is the basis of the wilderness. Somehow or other, in the economy of God a wilderness has a great relationship with sonship. It is a principle. "I went away into Arabia." What is Arabia? You do not get very much help from the world in Arabia, nor do you get very much help from the flesh. The flesh has nothing to thrive on in the desert; the natural life is starved in Arabia. You are alone with God: that is the point. Moses was alone with God in the desert for forty years. The Lord Jesus in the wilderness was alone with God. The Devil was there, it is true but He is now being tested and proved on this matter of His relationship with God without any help from the flesh or the world. Paul went away into Arabia. I have no doubt that during that time - some say two years - the sifting out of this position took place, the adjustment of things, the handing over of the old traditions to the new facts of experience. Perhaps you know something of Arabia.

You can live in a great city and be in Arabia. You may be here right in this meeting and be in Arabia at the same time. You are knowing something of the dry desert, the wilderness; that is, you are not finding a great deal upon which your natural life can thrive, a great deal to support you naturally in your relationship to the Lord. All that is being withdrawn, and you are coming to the place where it is the Lord, and only the Lord, and all other things are taken away. Beloved, the desert, Arabia, has proved again and again to be a school of sonship, and a very valuable school. Some of us know a little bit about Arabia. Oh, the desolation for the flesh there! "I conferred not with flesh and blood." No, it is coming, under desert conditions, to know the Lord. That is sonship, where the Lord alone is our resource, and where, if it were not for the Lord, we would die, our carcasses would fall in the wilderness; but we are proving that He can prepare a table in the wilderness. That is sonship. You will see the thing in principle and in spiritual meaning if you cannot follow or wholly grasp the way in which it is put. What the Lord is set upon is having us like that, sons in a true sense. May He have it so with us!

Chapter 5

THE MYSTERY OF THE GOSPEL

"... holding the mystery of the faith in a pure conscience" (1 Tim. 3:9).

"Only let your manner of life be worthy of the gospel of Christ: that, whether I come and see you and be absent, I may hear of your state, that ye stand fast in one spirit, with one soul striving for the faith of the gospel" (Phil. 1:27).

"... concerning his Son, who was born of the seed of David according to the flesh ... through whom we received grace and apostleship, unto obedience of faith among all the nations, for his name's sake ... Now to him that is able to establish you according to my gospel and the preaching of Jesus Christ, according to the revelation of the mystery which hath been kept in silence through times eternal, but now is manifested, and by the scriptures of the prophets, according to the commandment of the eternal God, is made known unto all the nations unto obedience of faith" (Rom. 1:3,5; 16:25-26)

"... how that by revelation was made known unto me the mystery, as I wrote before in few words, whereby, when ye read, ye can perceive my understanding in the mystery of Christ ... and to make all men see what is the dispensation of the mystery which for ages hath been hid in God who created all things ... till we all attain

unto the unity of the faith, and of the knowledge of the Son of God, unto a fullgrown man, unto the measure of the stature of the fulness of Christ" (Eph. 3:3-4,9; 4:13).

I think you will have recognised the familiar thoughts and words in all those passages, and the similar ideas. Some words stand out, such as Gospel, His Son, the mystery, the faith. They are all common words in those passages. And then, of course, there is the associated idea of conflict.

So this morning for a little while we are to be occupied with the mystery of the Gospel, or what the Gospel is. There is a very great need for a new apprehension of the nature of the Gospel. The Gospel has been very much reduced and whittled down, made merely to mean one or more of its parts, and its entirety, its fulness, has really been lost sight of. What I mean is, that so often the Gospel is said to be "the atoning work of the Lord Jesus", "righteousness which is by faith", "the forgiveness of sins"; all these things. All those things and many more like them are in the Gospel, they are parts of the Gospel, but the Gospel is something more than the parts. The Gospel is the sum of all those parts. But even then, when you have catalogued all the elements of the Gospel; God's redeeming love, forgiveness of sins, atonement for sin, when you have catalogued all the parts, you have still to get inside to know really what the Gospel is.

The Present Situation Amongst Christians

I am just wondering in these days - and we are all wondering and thinking very hard in the light of the situation - I am just wondering whether this may not be the matter upon which God is, to a very large extent, suspending operations today. I am just going to talk for a moment out of my heart, because I do feel that we are in a very perplexing, but very significant, situation at this time. There is a sense in which it does seem that the Lord is not doing very much. I mean there are no very manifest movements of God on the earth along certain lines in which we look for God to be moving. I do not mean that He is doing nothing, that there is nothing going on. I believe there is, and in parts a very real work of God going on. But, speaking generally, there is no great movement of God in an outward way spiritually. For a long time such forms of Divine activity seem to have been suspended. We think back to Wesley, and even to Moody, and then see that at a certain time a whole galaxy of great Bible teachers was raised up. We have all the names of the men of a generation ago. They have all gone. There are no movements like that, and have not been for a long time. Moreover the situation has changed so much that I do not believe that if all those men came back today, they could meet the situation. Something has happened. The situation has not only changed but it has become much deeper, and the need is for something more than has been during these past generations, something more potent and something deeper. The need is such as to require something from God of a new order. It was there, of course, in New Testament times. I am not thinking of something extra so far as the New Testament is concerned, but I am wondering very much whether this whole matter is not largely one of a new apprehension of what the Gospel is.

We have a very widespread situation the world over today amongst Christians which is an altogether unsatisfactory one, and I think most leaders and responsible people realise that. I think ministers and missionaries are aware that the state of the converts and the Christians is altogether unsatisfactory and inadequate. It is a real question sometimes whether many of them have really been born again. The spiritual life of the Lord's people is a very shallow thing, speaking generally, a very poor thing. And surely today it is manifest that the Church generally is failing to register itself with any impact upon the world situation. There is not a word, there is not a voice today for the present situation. You may gather leaders together on the present situation and no one has anything to say that really goes to the heart of matters. Why this apparent hiatus, this suspension of any general and impressive working, any working that is adequate to the situation, God seeming to be doing nothing? Oh, I believe that He is doing something inwardly, but that is not what I am talking about. Why does this situation obtain?

The Need for a New Apprehension of the Gospel

Well I say, I wonder whether it is not because there has to be a new apprehension of the Gospel. I believe that it really is the demand of a late hour in the dispensation; that we have advanced in this dispensation toward the end so much that the Lord cannot any longer accept the elementary. He must have the mature, He must have the fuller. Everything surely along the line of intensification as we see it demands that.

Now, of course, until His people have come to realise the ineffectiveness and the futility, the weakness and the failure of the partial, He cannot do anything; because the Lord always works with His people, and therefore He must have them in a state which makes it possible for Him to do something. If His people are content with something less, it would be a very unwise thing for Him to give His full thought in revelation. It would be perfectly useless. They would have no sense of need of it. May it not be that that is one of the deeper things He is doing, namely, creating and intensifying the sense of the weakness and futility of things, raising big questions even about the Gospel. I think there is reason to think that it is so. Thus it may be - I only put it in that form - that His answer is a new apprehension of the Gospel and what the Gospel is.

God's Secret

Now is it not interesting that here in the Scriptures you have such a phrase as this - "the mystery of the Gospel", and that word "mystery" is definitely stated to be a secret which God has deliberately held through ages and generations, an undisclosed, undivulged thought of His. He has verily in things throughout the ages deliberately kept a secret, had a secret, an unrevealed intention in relation to means and methods of reaching His end. And note again, it is not the mystery of some profound extra teaching, it is not that some revelation over and above the simple Gospel is the message. Oh, if that has got into your mind, get rid of it at once. The mystery is not some extra revelation of Divine truth, it is not something apart from the Gospel. I think a lot of people, when they hear words like those, "the mystery which hath been hid for ages", think that is higher truth, or something for people who are in another realm altogether from the ordinary person, that it is for some sort of spiritual aristocracy. No, it says here it is the *mystery of the Gospel.*

And then again the same word - "the mystery of Christ": and then, as we have noted, the bringing of these two things together, the Gospel of God concerning His Son, which is the mystery, the secret that had been hidden through all the ages and the generations, but which is now revealed: and Paul says, "my gospel".

Well now, what is this mystery of the Gospel which is the mystery of Christ, which is the mystery now disclosed? What is it? Can we put it into few words? We will try. In brief, the mystery is the incarnation of God in Christ in terms of sonship, with the intent that He should be the firstborn among many brethren, so that there shall be a Divine seed or family or Body. Oh, if we could but get inside of a statement like that! God's secret!

How did God decide to solve the whole problem of this universe after the chaos and ruin resultant from the working of Satan, and men's complicity with him, and the entrance of sin? How was God going to deal with this whole situation? By Himself coming right down in the form of man in terms of sonship and begetting a new race of beings as sharers of His own Divine life; not His Deity but His Divine life, partaking of His own Divine nature, becoming as a family, His own moral and spiritual reproduction in the universe. I say that is infinitely - may I use the word of God? - infinitely ingenious. There is wisdom about that that is profound. Not a working from the outside to try and remedy and patch up a broken down situation, not a dealing with the thing objectively at all but Himself coming right into it, God incarnate, God manifest in the flesh in terms of sonship; that is, in generic terms, to reproduce after His own kind. That is a secret which God kept hidden through ages and generations. God had that secret.

But how was He going to handle the whole thing? You can trace it now in the types and see it there. It is there in the tabernacle, in the ark of the testimony, it is there throughout the Old Testament in symbols. But they saw it not; God hid it. Now it is disclosed, the revelation is out. It is the mystery of the Gospel.

Sonship — the Occasion of the Conflict

What is the Gospel? It is Jesus Christ, God manifest in the flesh in terms of sonship, to generate a new race after His own kind, to bring many sons to glory. That is it in brief. Oh, that is something very much more than getting your sins forgiven, that is very much more than justification by faith. It is that, but it is infinitely more than that, and all the other things included; the deep, deep inner secret of God, how He is eventually going to have triumph in His original purpose; and what we have been seeing is this, that the faith is not a system of doctrine at all. The faith, according to the New Testament, is sonship, and it is in relation to sonship as an inward, spiritual reality brought about by this work of God in generation, it is that which is the occasion of all the conflict. The Son came and, right at His coming, hell was moved from beneath to withstand Him and to make His entrance into this world impossible, and to get Him out of it as soon as could be. All the way along it was upon this very point - "If thou be the Son..." Hear it in the wilderness, Satan saying, "If thou be the Son..." It is an assault upon sonship in terms of doubt, to try to paralyse the effect of that sonship by introducing some question about it. "If thou be the Son..." So it was all the way through; and then on the Cross you hear that Satanic hiss again, coming through the Jews who cried, "If thou be the Son of God, come down from the cross" (Matt. 27:40). Only when we are in conditions and circumstances of extreme pressure and adversity, only then are we able to understand a little of what it meant to have that question raised at such a time. *You* the Son of God! Poor Son of God! Look at you, look at your condition, look at your situation! God has left you! This is the outworking of your own foolish ways, your own self-chosen way; there is no trace of sonship about this! "If thou be the Son..." - raising the question again in the light of the awful conditions. It is the assault upon sonship.

And then the assault was transferred from the Son to His seed, and we know quite well that the real nature of spiritual conflict is not around our creed, our profession; it is over the spiritual life that is in us. It is about that mystery in us of a difference. We are going the same way as He went, we are being subjected to the testing fires of adversity. The Lord allows conditions to arise in our lives which seem wholeheartedly to deny that we are sons, that we have been born out from God, that God is with us, that God is in us by His Spirit. All the conditions seem at times to put God far from us, and there is nothing whatever to argue that we are sons. That is the test of faith.

And the faith is just that; not only faith in Him but the faith is that we are sons, sons of God, in the midst of a wicked and perverse generation, in the midst of a world that is hostile, in the midst of a cosmos full of antagonistic spirits. Yes, the fact of sonship is there through new birth, but sonship is something more than birth, sonship is maturity. That is where the consideration at this time comes in. It is so clear that the New Testament shows that the continuation unto the full growth of sonship is as vital and as important as the beginning of sonship; that is, the bringing of the Lord's people to full spiritual growth is as important as bringing them to new birth. That is where there has been a breakdown.

That brings us right back to what I was saying at the beginning. Today, and for a long time, evangelical leaders have put all the emphasis, or the main emphasis, upon getting people saved. They are interested in that more than anything else, and that is the direction of their main occupation. With what result? That we see a most unsatisfactory state among Christians, and that too in the face of the fact that the very existence of the New Testament itself is the evidence that to bring converted people to full spiritual growth is as important as bringing them to new birth. Why have we the New Testament, with Corinthians, Galatians, Ephesians, Philippians, Colossians, and all the other letters, occupied with the fight of the faith to bring believers to full growth? Every one of them is a battleground.

Look at Paul's fight for Galatia. What a fight it was against those Judaizers who had come in, and were causing arrest to the spiritual progress of the believers there. Paul had to say, "I marvel that you are so soon removed... unto another gospel". Hebrews is another battleground. All these letters are battlegrounds, and they all have to do, not with the conversion of the unsaved but the going on of the saved, the terrific fight of sonship. Why? Because the issue is not that babes are going to oust the powers of darkness, but full-grown believers. The Church has to come to maturity.

So the Apostle says, "When he ascended on high, he led captivity captive, and gave gifts unto men... and he gave some apostles: and some, prophets"; and so on. What for? "The perfecting of the saints... till we all attain unto the unity of the faith... unto a full-grown man, unto the measure of the stature of the fulness of Christ" (Eph. 4:8,11-13). The unity of the faith, the fulness of Christ. You see, that is the thing that comes to light. It is just as important for the seed or the family or the Body to come to spiritual full-growth as it is for it to be begotten at all. That is a tremendous thing. The mystery of the Gospel is not just getting people born again. The mystery of the Gospel is the fulness of Christ, and that only begins at new birth. This is the disclosed secret, this Gospel, and it is the occasion of the tremendous, unrelenting conflict, a cosmic conflict with principalities, powers, world-rulers of this darkness, spiritual hosts of wickedness in the heavenlies (Eph. 6:12). That is where the wrestling goes on.

The Focal Point of the Conflict – Its Nature and Outcome

With one word of emphasis, I close for the present. Beloved, the focal point of the conflict is the spiritual advancement of the children of God toward full-growth, and by any means whatever the enemy will seek to interfere with that. He is striking right at the heart of this thing all the time by every means in his power. God will reach His end, He will come in, in His Son in terms of sonship, to take up residence within those begotten of Him, and will grow in them, increase His measure in them, until at last, brought to the unity of the faith, they become a mighty embodiment and revelation of God Himself; not in Deity, but in what He is spiritually and morally in this universe, conformed to the image of His Son, a living expression of God's own thoughts, to fill His universe. The enemy is out against that, and every little step in that direction is challenged, the spiritual growth is countered all the time. He is striking at God's Son. Of course in principle it is quite true that the fight rages round the person of the Lord Jesus. There is a great fight going on between modernism and fundamentalism. The one stands on the ground of the absolute Deity of Christ, Christ manifest in the flesh, and the others will not have it. So the fight rages. But that is an objective fight really, a fight of creeds, philosophies, ideologies. It does not get very far spiritually. I grieve to think that some of the most unspiritual and unkind and unChristlike people have been the most rabid fundamentalists who would fight to the death for the Deity of Christ. It does not get you very far spiritually. It is something more than that, is His Deity. You see what I mean. It goes deeper than that.

The person of the Lord Jesus means something more than what He is in Himself as one apart. It is what He is in this life of sonship as manifested in believers. God manifest in the flesh is not something in the way of a creed to be argued out. God manifest in the flesh is something to be proved by a life. I do not know but that it may have a meaning, that Jesus Christ came into this world and was Emmanuel, God with us, that God did incarnate Himself in that Man, and did some things, and went back to heaven. It might mean something, but I do not know that it would get me very far as something back there. If that fact of God in Christ did not become some reality right at the centre of my life, it would lack something of real value. The mystery is this - "Christ in you, the hope of glory" (Col. 1:27). It is the same mystery. There are not a half a dozen mysteries in the New Testament. It is the Gospel of God concerning His Son, and the Gospel is not a system of truth to be preached, the Gospel is a Person, and the power of the Gospel is not that you accept certain things proposed to you about Jesus Christ, but that Jesus Christ comes to reside in you by new birth. That is the Gospel. That, of course, is going back to the very elementary; but oh, that we could get a fresh glimpse of the immense significance of the Gospel, the Gospel of God concerning His Son, Jesus Christ, God's secret! I like to dwell upon that. If you sit down in the presence of the world situation and try to sort it out and find the solution to it, it is beyond us, altogether; but all through the ages God has been perfectly at rest about this whole thing, about the issue. He was able to say, I have the secret of the whole thing, I have solved the whole problem, I have the means in hand; in the end My method will absolutely succeed! And the secret? - why it is just this: I will go down Myself in terms of sonship and will generate a new race through faith, and that new race will be brought eventually to spiritual full-growth; which simply means that then I shall fill all, I shall occupy all the space; there will be no room for anything else at all! That is the issue for every Christian life. It is whether God is going to fill the whole space or not, or whether we are going to have a bit. All the time that is what is going on. Can the Lord gain the ground, will we give way to Him? Are we holding the ground for ourselves, are we in His way? Are we going to let the Lord have all the territory of our being in every way. It is not so easy as saying, Yes! It becomes a daily challenge. There is a strong, many-sided, subtle self-life. We never know how difficult it is to let the Lord have His way until He lights upon some pet opinion of our self-life. But that is the issue. When the Lord has gained His full way in all His own, as He will at the end, the manifestation of the sons of God will take place, and the whole problem will have been solved, the problem of this universe.

To see the entire LIFE SENTENCE Publishing booklist, go to our website: www.lifesentencepublishing.com, or request a booklist and order form from:

LIFE SENTENCE Publishing, LLC
404 N 5th Street
Abbotsford, WI 54405